ORAL LANGUAGE

Written by Graeme Beals
Illustrated by Peter Humbert

World Teachers Press

Published with the permission of R.I.C. Publications Pty. Ltd.

Copyright © 1997 by Didax, Inc., Rowley, MA 01969. All rights reserved.

First published by R.I.C. Publications Pty. Ltd., Perth, Western Australia.

Printed in the United States of America.

Order Number 2-5041
ISBN 1-885111-54-1

B C D E F 97 98 99

Educational Resources

395 Main Street
Rowley, MA 01969

INTRODUCTION

Language programs generally emphasize the development of reading and writing skills, yet we are often judged on our ability to speak and listen.

The activities in **Oral Language** promote oral language skills, placing emphasis on the ability of students to listen with understanding and to respond orally in a confident, coherent manner.

Activities are based on the premise that skills in this area require constant practice to build both proficiency and confidence.

As all activities involve working in pairs or groups, students are required to operate in a cooperative manner. This provides an ideal environment in which less confident students are able to develop their skills.

The activities can be used as occasional exercises, as a daily practice session, or as part of a complete theme of work: for example, when studying a topic where communicating accurate information is pertinent, such as map reading.

The sheets enable teachers to assess each student's accuracy and improvement in oral tasks.

Only by regularly providing students the opportunity to practice and to develop the skills of listening and speaking, will they achieve their full potential in the future.

CONTENTS

Teacher Information

Introduction

Oral language is an area of learning that is often assumed as occurring throughout the daily teaching program and in general life. This series of three blackline masters provides the opportunity to focus on the specific skills of oral language and to both teach and identify areas of weakness in students. This focus is important for both students and teachers.

The series is developmental as it requires an increased level of skill both within each book and throughout the series. Each book is divided into three sections:

Set 1. Student A adjusting a picture and communicating the adjustments to student B;

Set 2. Description and drawing from memory; and

Set 3. Using questions to gain specific information.

Each section develops an area of oral language that is specific and provides a range of activities to develop and consolidate skills in that area.

As with all oral language skills there is an aspect of listening skills that is developed as part of the process.

For more specific listening skills activities, refer to the series *Listen! Hear!*

Set 1 - pages 6-13

Preparation for this activity is important. Students must understand the task clearly and then be sure their communication is clear and explicit when talking to their partner. Explain to the students that the success of their partner depends greatly on the quality of their own communication. The following sets of activities further develop this skill. In addition, these activities can be repeated by using a variety of different drawings, photographs, magazine pictures, etc. The placement of crosses by each student needs to be accurate.

Accurate placement of crosses is necessary.

Think before you speak. Plan your instruction.

Provide criteria for accuracy.

Important for both students to have a turn in each role.

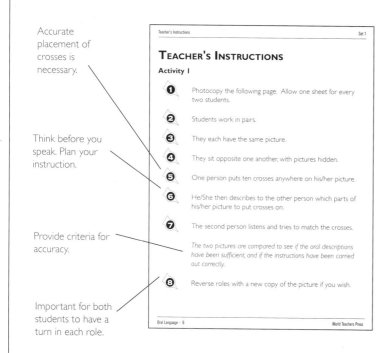

Teacher Information

Set 2 - pages 14-21

The point to emphasize with this style of activity, as with most oral communication, is that students should take their time. Time to think about what they are going to say as well as time to actually communicate. Students could plan their communication before commencing. The repeated use of this style of activity will highlight the need for accuracy.

Have students plan their communication.

Encourage students to sequence their instruction to make the drawing of the page easier.

Drawings need to be accurate and in one color.

A level of leniency needs to be factored in to account for drawing ability.

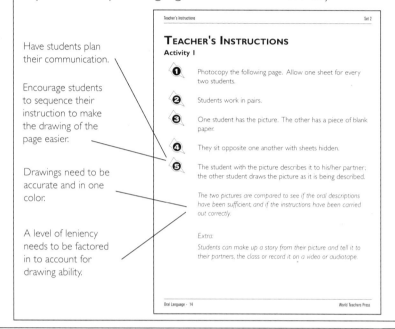

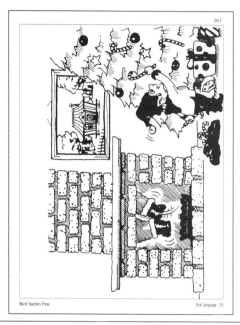

Set 3 - pages 22-29

This activity type focuses on the importance of questioning. It encourages students to think about their questions so they elicit maximum information with a minimal amount of questioning. Again, time and planning will achieve the best results. Students should ensure questions provide for a yes/no answer.

Questions should be specific.

Students should organize their picture into sections and plan their questions accordingly.

It may be necessary to place a time limit.

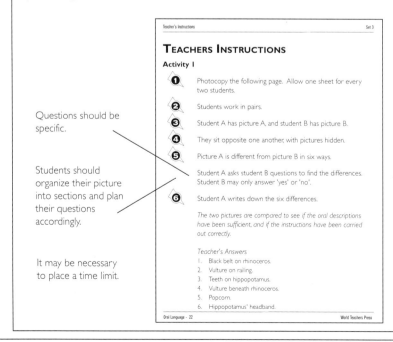

TEACHER'S INSTRUCTIONS

Activity 1

 Photocopy the following page. Allow one sheet for every two students.

 Students work in pairs.

 They each have the same picture.

 They sit opposite one another, with pictures hidden.

 One person puts ten crosses anywhere on his/her picture.

 He/She then describes to the other person which parts of his/her picture to put crosses on.

 The second person listens and tries to match the crosses.

The two pictures are compared to see if the oral descriptions have been sufficient, and if the instructions have been carried out correctly.

 Reverse roles with a new copy of the picture if you wish.

TEACHER'S INSTRUCTIONS

Activity 3

 Photocopy the following page. Allow one sheet for every two students.

 Students work in pairs.

 They each have the same picture.

 They sit opposite one another, with pictures hidden.

 One person makes ten additions or alterations to his/her picture.

 He/She then describes these changes for the other person to try to copy.

The two pictures are compared to see if the oral descriptions have been sufficient, and if the instructions have been carried out correctly.

 Reverse roles with a new copy of the picture if you wish.
Suggestions for the students to draw:
- *Dragon*
- *Queen*
- *Horse*
- *Flags on the castle*

Teacher's Instructions

Activity 4

 Photocopy the following page. Allow one sheet for every two students.

 Students work in pairs.

 They each have the same picture.

 They sit opposite one another, with pictures hidden.

 One person draws five lines. Each line joins two objects in the picture. Lines start and finish at certain points on the objects. Lines can go in any direction.

 That person gives the start and finish points to his/her partner so that he/she knows where to draw the lines.

The two pictures are compared to see if the oral descriptions have been sufficient, and if the instructions have been carried out correctly.

 Reverse roles with a new copy of the picture if you wish.

TEACHER'S INSTRUCTIONS
Activity 1

 Photocopy the following page. Allow one sheet for every two students.

 Students work in pairs.

 One student has the picture. The other has a piece of blank paper.

 They sit opposite one another, with sheets hidden.

 The student with the picture describes it to his/her partner; the other student draws the picture as it is being described.

The two pictures are compared to see if the oral descriptions have been sufficient, and if the instructions have been carried out correctly.

Extra:

Students can make up a story from their picture and tell it to their partners, the class, or record it on a video or audiotape.

TEACHER'S INSTRUCTIONS

Activity 2

 Photocopy the following page. Allow one sheet for every two students.

 Students work in pairs.

 One student has a picture. The other has a piece of blank paper.

 They sit opposite one another, with sheets hidden.

 The student with the picture describes it.

 When the description is completed, the listener draws the picture from his/her memory.

The two pictures are compared to see if the oral descriptions have been sufficient, and if the instructions have been carried out correctly.

Extra:

Students can make up a story from their picture and tell it to their partners, the class, or record it on a video or audiotape.

TEACHER'S INSTRUCTIONS

Activity 3

 Photocopy the following page. Allow one sheet for every two students.

 Students work in pairs.

 One student has the picture.

 They sit so the picture is hidden from one partner.

 The student with the picture describes it to the other.

 The second student then describes it from memory on a tape.

 Play the description back and see if it matches the picture.

The two pictures are compared to see if the oral descriptions have been sufficient, and if the instructions have been carried out correctly.

Extra:

Students can make up a story from their picture and tell it to their partners, the class, or record it on a video or audiotape.

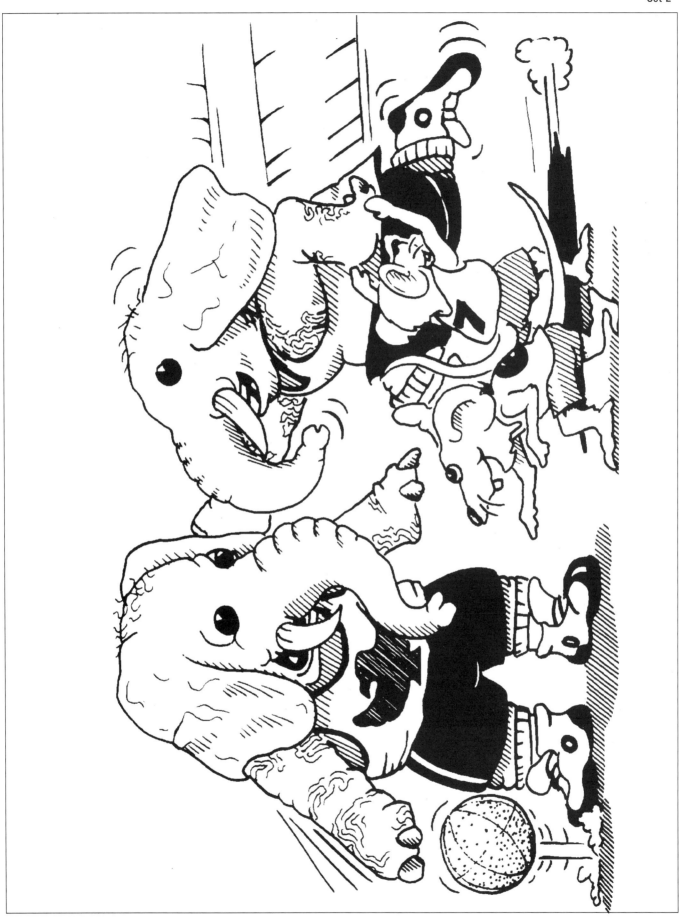

TEACHER'S INSTRUCTIONS
Activity 4

 Photocopy the following page. Allow one sheet for every three students.

 Students work in threes.

 The first student has the picture. The second a piece of blank paper, and the third student has nothing.

 They sit so the sheets of paper are hidden from one another, and so the third student cannot hear the first student.

 The first student describes the picture to the second student, who then describes it to the third student.

 The third student draws the picture from the second student's description.

The two pictures are compared to see if the oral descriptions have been sufficient, and if the instructions have been carried out correctly.

Extra:

Students can make up a story from their picture and tell it to their partners, the class, or record it on a video or audiotape.

TEACHER'S INSTRUCTIONS

Activity 1

 Photocopy the following page. Allow one sheet for every two students.

 Students work in pairs.

 Student A has picture A, and student B has picture B.

 They sit opposite one another, with pictures hidden.

 Picture A is different from picture B in six ways.

Student A asks student B questions to find the differences. Student B may only answer 'yes' or 'no'.

 Student A writes down the six differences.

The two pictures are compared to see if the oral descriptions have been sufficient, and if the instructions have been carried out correctly.

Teacher's Answers

1.   Black belt on rhinoceros.
2.   Vulture on railing.
3.   Teeth on hippopotamus.
4.   Vulture beneath rhinoceros.
5.   Popcorn.
6.   Hippopotamus' headband.

TEACHER'S INSTRUCTIONS

Activity 2

 Photocopy the following page. Allow one sheet for every two students.

 Students work in pairs.

 Student A has picture A, and student B has picture B.

 They sit opposite one another, with pictures hidden.

 Student B asks student A questions to find six differences between the pictures. Student A may only answer 'yes' or 'no'.

 Student B alters his/her picture to match picture A.

The two pictures are compared to see if the oral descriptions have been sufficient, and if the instructions have been carried out correctly.

Teacher's Answers

1. Number '5's on front car.
2. Ticket stand 'Ticket(s)'.
3. Missing headlight.
4. Baskets on ferris wheel.
5. Flag on tent.
6. Boy's hair color.

TEACHER'S INSTRUCTIONS

Activity 3

 Photocopy the following page. Allow one sheet for every two students.

 Students work in pairs.

 Student A has picture A, and student B has picture B.

 They sit opposite one another, with pictures hidden.

 Student B asks student A questions to find six differences between the pictures. Student A may only answer 'yes' or 'no'.

 Student B alters his/her picture to match picture A.

The two pictures are compared to see if the oral descriptions have been sufficient, and if the instructions have been carried out correctly.

Teacher's Answers

1. Dresser handles.
2. Spray can.
3. Earring.
4. Numbers on telephone.
5. Socks on girl.
6. Letter on poster.

TEACHER'S INSTRUCTIONS

Activity 4

 Photocopy the following page. Allow one sheet for every two students.

 Students work in pairs.

 Student A has picture A, and student B has picture B.

 They sit opposite one another, with pictures hidden.

 Student A asks student B questions to find six differences between the pictures. Student B may only answer 'yes' or 'no'.

 Student A alters his/her picture to match picture B.

The two pictures are compared to see if the oral descriptions have been sufficient, and if the instructions have been carried out correctly.

Teacher's Answers

1. Card on box.
2. Clock hand.
3. Knight near box.
4. Windows on tower.
5. Television.
6. Missing tree from gameboard.

About the Author

SOUTH PACIFIC OCEAN

TASMAN SEA

NEW ZEALAND

NORTH ISLAND

SOUTH ISLAND

WELLINGTON

Graeme Beals, New Plymouth, New Zealand.
Graeme is a New Zealand primary school teacher and educational publisher.
He has spent many years in classroom, advisory and administrative positions
in New Zealand schools. His books are noted for their unique approach to
learning and their ability to target skill areas that often benefit from specific
focus and attention. Graeme now runs a successful publishing house in New
Zealand.